CELEBRATING THE NAME JAMES

Celebrating the Name James

Walter the Educator

Silent King Books a WhichHead Imprint

Copyright © 2024 by Walter the Educator

All rights reserved. No part of this book may be reproduced in any manner whatsoever without written permission except in the case of brief quotations embodied in critical articles and reviews.

First Printing, 2024

Disclaimer
This book is a literary work; poems are not about specific persons, locations, situations, and/or circumstances unless mentioned in a historical context. This book is for entertainment and informational purposes only. The author and publisher offer this information without warranties expressed or implied. No matter the grounds, neither the author nor the publisher will be accountable for any losses, injuries, or other damages caused by the reader's use of this book. The use of this book acknowledges an understanding and acceptance of this disclaimer.

dedicated to everyone with the first name of James

"Earning a degree in chemistry changed my life and gave me a respect for the discipline of poetry." - Walter the Educator

Chemistry and poetry may seem disparate, yet a nuanced exploration reveals an intriguing interplay between the empirical realm of molecules and the ethereal domain of verses. At first glance, chemistry delves into the molecular tapestry of existence, unraveling the secrets of elements and compounds. Conversely, poetry ventures into the boundless realms of emotions and imagination, weaving linguistic tapestries that transcend the physical confines.

Upon closer inspection, parallels emerge. Both disciplines involve a meticulous dance of elements—whether in the periodic table or the rhythmic patterns of language. The periodicity of elements resonates with the cadence of poetic meter, each element possessing a unique identity, akin to the distinct essence of words. Chemical reactions, akin to the fusion of words in verses, engender transformative experiences.

Metaphors and similes, intrinsic to poetic expression, find an unexpected ally in chemistry's ability to draw parallels between disparate phenomena. The alchemy of language mirrors the transformative processes witnessed in chemical reactions, where the mundane metamorphoses into the extraordinary.

In essence, chemistry and poetry converge at the crossroads of creativity, where one seeks the essence of matter, and the other, the essence of expression. The alchemical union of these seemingly divergent realms births a synthesis of understanding, inviting us to perceive the world through the kaleidoscopic lens of both science and art.

CONTENTS

Dedication v

One - Grace And Power 1

Two - In Every Name 3

Three - Steadfast And Strong 5

Four - Oh, James 7

Five - History's Flame 9

Six - Hall Of Fame 11

Seven - Valor And Might 13

Eight - Linguistic Wonderland 14

Nine - Jubilant James 16

Ten - Jocund James 18

Eleven - Forever Celebrated 20

Twelve - Name That Stands Out 22

Thirteen - Proudly Shown 24

Fourteen - Honor James 26

Fifteen - Celebrate James 28

Sixteen - James, The Legend 30

Seventeen - James, The Wanderer 32

Eighteen - The Oracle Of Poetic Seas 34

Nineteen - James, The Luminary 36

Twenty - James, The Poet Laureate 38

Twenty-One - Poetic Masterpiece 40

Twenty-Two - Love And Might 42

Twenty-Three - Forever Reign 44

Twenty-Four - For In James 46

Twenty-Five - Eternally Bright 48

Twenty-Six - Sanctified Place 50

Twenty-Seven - Dispels The Gloom 52

Twenty-Eight - Brilliance Entwines 54

Twenty-Nine - Kaleidoscope Of Words . . . 56

Thirty - James, We Acclaim 58

Thirty-One - Forever In Name 60

Thirty-Two - Dance Of Letters 62

Thirty-Three - Radiant Star 64

Thirty-Four - Rare And Fair 66

Thirty-Five - Every Soul 68

About The Author 70

ONE

GRACE AND POWER

In the realm of names, one stands tall,
James, a moniker beloved by all.
A name of kings and noble knights,
A beacon of strength, a shining light.

From ancient times to modern days,
James has earned its rightful praise.
A name of honor, courage, and might,
Guiding hearts through the darkest night.

With each syllable, a tale is told,
Of valor, wisdom, and stories bold.
From fields of battle to halls of fame,
James, forever etched in history's frame.

Oh, James, a name so strong and true,
A melody whispered by the morning dew.
A name that echoes through the ages,
Written in the lore of countless pages.

So here's to James, in prose and rhyme,
A timeless emblem, standing the test of time.
A name that rings with grace and power,
In every triumph, in every hour.

TWO

IN EVERY NAME

In a world of names, one shines bright,
James, a symphony of pure delight.
A name that dances on the lips of fate,
A melody that none can replicate.
From dawn's first light to twilight's gleam,
James, a name that sparks a dream.
A name that whispers of mystery untold,
A tapestry of secrets, a saga to behold.
With each letter, a universe unfurls,
A cosmic journey, like precious pearls.
From galaxies afar to oceans deep,
James, a name that never falls asleep.
Oh, James, a name so rich with lore,
A treasure trove of wonders to explore.
A name that paints the sky with hues,
A kaleidoscope of ever-changing views.

So here's to James, a name of endless quest,
A boundless spirit, on a timeless quest.
A name that weaves through destiny's frame,
In every heartbeat, in every name.

THREE

STEADFAST AND STRONG

Amidst a chorus of names, one stands tall,
James, a beacon of resilience through it all.
A name that weathers the storms of time,
A symphony of strength in every climb.
From the ashes of trials, James arises,
A name that echoes through endless guises.
A testament to fortitude and grace,
Guiding souls to find their rightful place.
With each heartbeat, a tale takes flight,
Of triumph over darkness, of unwavering might.
From valleys low to peaks so high,
James, a name that dares to touch the sky.
Oh, James, a name that carries the flame,
A phoenix reborn, never to be the same.

A name that heralds a spirit unbound,
In every echo, in every sound.
    So here's to James, in whispers and song,
A name that marches steadfast and strong.
A name that blooms in fields of change,
In every chapter, in every range.

FOUR

OH, JAMES

Amidst the tapestry of names, one shines bright,
James, a legacy woven with celestial might.
A name that echoes through history's grand hall,
A timeless anthem, embracing one and all.

From ancient kingdoms to modern-day lore,
James, a name revered, cherished evermore.
A symphony of triumph, a saga untold,
Guiding hearts with stories of courage so bold.

With each syllable, a legend unfolds,
Of honor, wisdom, and tales untold.
From ancient scrolls to future's embrace,
James, a name that leaves an eternal trace.

Oh, James, a name that etches the stars,
A legacy that transcends earthly bars.
A name that resonates through time's embrace,
In every heartbeat, in every place.

So here's to James, in history's embrace,
A name that stands with unwavering grace.
A name that weaves through destiny's frame,
In every legacy, in every acclaim.

FIVE

HISTORY'S FLAME

In the tapestry of names, one gleams with might,
James, a compass guiding through day and night.
A name that whispers of journeys untold,
A melody of adventure, courageous and bold.
From distant shores to mountains high,
James, a name that yearns to touch the sky.
A symphony of discovery, a tale of the brave,
Igniting flames in every heart that craves.
With each letter, a quest takes flight,
Of quests and conquests, in dawn and twilight.
From uncharted seas to lands afar,
James, a name that echoes like a shooting star.
Oh, James, a name that sparks the flame,
A legacy of explorers, never the same.
A name that charts the course of fate,
In every wanderer, in every mate.

So here's to James, in adventures untold,
A name that sails through legends bold.
A name that roars through history's flame,
In every journey, in every name.

SIX

HALL OF FAME

Amidst the symphony of life, James shines bright,
A name that resonates with undying might.
A melody of resilience, a saga of grace,
Guiding souls through every trial they face.
From ancient tales to modern days,
James, a name that weaves through time's maze.
A tapestry of valor, a legend so true,
Inspiring hearts with all that it can imbue.
With each syllable, a story is spun,
Of battles fought and victories won.
From whispers in the wind to the lion's roar,
James, a name that echoes forevermore.
Oh, James, a name that stands the test,
A legacy of courage, of giving your best.
A name that paints the sky with hues,
In every triumph, in every muse.

So here's to James, in whispers and cheer,
A name that triumphs over every fear.
A name that etches its mark in the hall of fame,
In every chapter, in every name.

SEVEN

VALOR AND MIGHT

In the realm of names, one shines bright,
James, a beacon of strength and light.
A symphony of echoes from ages past,
Guiding souls with a wisdom that will always last.
With each syllable, a legacy is told,
Of honor, resilience, and stories bold.
From ancient chronicles to modern days,
James, a name that forever stays.
Oh, James, a name that stands so tall,
A fortress of hope, never to fall.
A name that resonates through history's grace,
In every journey, in every embrace.
So here's to James, in valor and might,
A name that blazes through the darkest night.
A name that weaves through destiny's flame,
In every heartbeat, in every acclaim.

EIGHT

LINGUISTIC WONDERLAND

In the realm of names, a gem does shine,
James, a symphony, pure and divine.
A melody woven in letters so grand,
Resonating through the vast name-land.

In the tapestry of linguistic grace,
James takes its place, a poetic embrace.
A symposium of syllables, a linguistic ballet,
In the lexicon, it dances, forever to stay.

Jubilant James, a sonorous decree,
Echoing through time, a linguistic spree.
Each letter, a brushstroke on the canvas of sound,
In the name's symphony, a resonance profound.

Jovial and jocular, a linguistic delight,
James, a beacon in the language's twilight.

Juxtaposed with others, it stands alone,
A linguistic masterpiece, on language's throne.
    Journey through the lexicon, hand in hand,
With James, a linguistic wonderland.
A jubilant journey, a poetic flight,
In the name's embrace, language takes flight.

NINE

JUBILANT JAMES

In the realm of appellations, a jewel to acclaim,
James, a moniker with an illustrious flame.
A linguistic ballet, a harmonious trance,
In the lexicon's ballroom, James does dance.
  Jubilant echoes through syllabic delight,
James, a melody in the linguistic twilight.
A sonorous sonnet, a lyrical spree,
In the vast name-scape, it reigns with glee.
  Juxtaposed with consonants, vowels in a duet,
James, a linguistic silhouette.
Each phoneme, a brushstroke, strokes of art,
In the gallery of names, a masterpiece's part.
  Jovial resonance, a symphony's hum,
In the name's embrace, language becomes.
A journey through syllables, a poetic quest,
James, a linguistic marvel, distinct from the rest.

Jubilant James, in alphabetical array,
A name that sparkles, come what may.
In the tapestry of language, an embroidered frame,
James, forever celebrated, in the lexicon's acclaim.

TEN

JOCUND JAMES

In the lexicon's theater, a star takes the stage,
James, the protagonist on language's page.
A sonnet of syllables, a lyrical spree,
In the grand symphony of names, it's the key.
Jovial James, a linguistic serenade,
Each letter, a dancer in the phonetic parade.
Juxtaposed with vowels and consonant grace,
In the linguistic tapestry, it finds its place.
Journey through echoes of phonetic delight,
James, a melody in the language's light.
A jubilant journey through syllabic art,
In the name's embrace, a linguistic heart.
Jubilant resonance, a symphony's tune,
In the linguistic garden, a vibrant monsoon.
A juxtaposition of sounds, a harmonious play,
James, the maestro leading the linguistic array.

Jocund James, a poetic expedition,
Through vowels and consonants in rhythmic condition.
In the name's narrative, a linguistic revelation,
James, a lexicon's celebrated creation.

ELEVEN

FOREVER CELEBRATED

In the vast expanse of linguistic lore,
James emerges, a name to adore.
A symphony of syllables, a rhythmic trance,
In the realm of words, it does enhance.
    Jovial James, a linguistic cascade,
Each letter a dancer in a poetic parade.
Juxtaposed with vowels, consonants in a ballet,
In the tapestry of language, it holds sway.
    Jubilant echoes through the phonetic breeze,
James, a melody that effortlessly appease.
A sonorous sonnet, a lyrical spree,
In the lexicon's ballroom, dancing free.
    Juxtaposition of sounds, a harmonious blend,
James, the maestro, leading language to transcend.

A journey through phonetic landscapes vast,
In the name's embrace, a linguistic contrast.
    Jocular James, in the alphabet's embrace,
A linguistic gem, standing with grace.
In the symphony of names, a prominent chord,
James, forever celebrated, in language adored.

TWELVE

NAME THAT STANDS OUT

In the tapestry of linguistic tales,
James emerges, a name that never pales.
A harmonious dance of syllabic delight,
In the lexicon's garden, it takes flight.

Jovial James, a lyrical symphony,
Each letter a note in linguistic harmony.
Juxtaposed with vowels, a poetic blend,
In the name's narrative, a journey to attend.

Jubilant echoes through the phonetic air,
James, a melody beyond compare.
A sonorous sonnet, a rhythmic spree,
In the vast expanse of language, it roams free.

Juxtaposition of consonants and vowels,
James, a linguistic marvel that enthralls.

Jocular and jubilant, in language's embrace,
A name that stands out, leaving a trace.
   Journey through syllabic landscapes grand,
In the linguistic symposium, James takes command.
A linguistic gem, radiant and bright,
In the lexicon's constellation, a guiding light.

THIRTEEN

PROUDLY SHOWN

In lands afar and realms untold,
Where tales of valor are often told,
There lived a man of noble fame,
James was the glory of his name.
With courage bold and heart so true,
His spirit soared the wide world through,
In every challenge, he found his way,
James, the beacon, in night and day.
From ancient times to modern days,
The name of James forever stays,
A legacy of honor and might,
Guiding souls through darkest night.
In laughter's echo and sorrow's wail,
James stood firm, he did not fail,
A name that rings with timeless charm,
In history's embrace, a soothing balm.

So raise a toast to James, the great,
Whose legend we commemorate,
For in his name, we find our own,
A legacy of love, proudly shown.

FOURTEEN

HONOR JAMES

In fields of gold and skies so wide,
A name resounds with endless pride,
James, the bearer of noble might,
In whose name, we find our light.

With wisdom vast and spirit free,
James charts a course across the sea,
A name that echoes through the ages,
In history's book, its story rages.

Through trials fierce and battles won,
James stands tall, a radiant sun,
A name that sparks the flame of hope,
In every heart, a boundless scope.

From dawn's first blush to twilight's gleam,
James, a vision, a timeless dream,
A name that whispers in the breeze,
A symphony that knows no cease.

So let us honor James today,
In every word and deed we say,
For in his name, we find our way,
A guiding star that will not sway.

FIFTEEN

CELEBRATE JAMES

In realms of valor and tales untold,
A name shines bright, a story bold,
James, a beacon through history's page,
A name that transcends each era and age.

With courage as vast as the endless sea,
James forges ahead, bold and free,
A name that echoes through time's embrace,
A symbol of strength, a spirit's grace.

In moments of triumph and trials untamed,
James stands unwavering, unashamed,
A name that whispers in the wind,
A legacy of fortitude, beautifully thinned.

From the fields of honor to the halls of might,
James' name blazes a trail, shining bright,
A name that resonates with boundless power,
In every soul, in every hour.

So let us celebrate James, the name so true,
In its essence, we find courage anew,
For in its letters, a story unfolds,
Of resilience, of grace, of tales untold.

SIXTEEN

JAMES, THE LEGEND

In realms of time where echoes dance,
A name resounds, a sweet romance.
James, the symphony of strength,
In whispers, tales of valor length.
  Beneath the azure, where dreams alight,
James, a beacon, a celestial light.
With each syllable, a cosmic spark,
Igniting galaxies in the cosmic dark.
  In meadows of language, blooms his grace,
James, a melody, a sonnet's embrace.
Through pages penned by fate's own hand,
His name, a treasure in love's grandstand.
  Bold as the lion in twilight's gleam,
James, the architect of a poet's dream.
In letters woven, a tapestry unfolds,
A timeless saga, where his story molds.

    Within the heart, where emotions flow,
James, a river, an eternal glow.
Majestic echoes in every verse,
His name, a blessing, a universe.
    So here we sing, in poetic flame,
James, the legend, an immortal name.
A kaleidoscope of words we weave,
In homage to the one, whom we believe.

SEVENTEEN

JAMES, THE WANDERER

Beneath the moonlit tapestry of cosmic art,
James, a sonnet written on the heart.
In the dance of stardust, his name ascends,
A celestial echo that forever transcends.
Within the garden of linguistic delight,
James, a bloom that paints the night.
A quasar of syllables, a meteor's flight,
His name, a comet in the poet's sight.
A serenade whispered by the zephyr's breath,
James, the rhythm of life and death.
A phoenix soaring through time's embrace,
His name, an anthem in the vast space.
Through the labyrinth of language's maze,
James, a constellation ablaze.

A symphony composed in ink and quill,
His name, a melody that time can't still.
    With the might of mountains, sturdy and strong,
James, a ballad in nature's song.
In the kaleidoscope of existence, a radiant hue,
His name, a prism painting the view.
    So let the verses weave a tapestry rare,
James, the wanderer in the poetic air.
In the lexicon of dreams, an eternal flame,
His name, a masterpiece without a frame.

EIGHTEEN

THE ORACLE OF POETIC SEAS

In the realm of syllabic serenity, James unfolds,
A symphony of letters, a story untold.
Where echoes of antiquity softly chime,
James, the poet's quill, in rhythmic rhyme.

Beneath the crescent moon's silver sheen,
His name, a whispered sonnet, unseen.
A tapestry woven with threads divine,
James, the mystic word, an opulent sign.

Through the labyrinth of language, he strides,
James, the harbinger where eloquence abides.
In the cosmic dance of ink and air,
His name, a constellation beyond compare.

A cascade of verses, a cascade of stars,
James, the celestial bard, leaving no memoirs.

With each syllable, an odyssey begins,
His name, an anthem as the universe spins.
　In the lexicon of dreams, a beacon aglow,
James, the artisan of words in a cosmic flow.
A melody etched in the scrolls of time,
His name, a timeless rhythm, sublime.
　So let the quill dance in the midnight breeze,
James, the oracle of poetic seas.
In the mosaic of language, a portrait unfurls,
His name, a verse that forever twirls.

NINETEEN

JAMES, THE LUMINARY

In the theater of language, where narratives bloom,
James graces the stage, dispelling gloom.
A linguistic alchemist, his name a potion,
In the enchanted verses, a lyrical ocean.
Beneath the celestial canopy of ink and quill,
James, the maestro, orchestrating skill.
A magnum opus in the poet's hand,
His name, a melody across the land.
Through the epochs of time, a resounding echo,
James, the echo in history's meadow.
A constellation in the vast expanse,
His name, a celestial dance.
In the garden of prose, a perennial bloom,
James, the fragrance in language's room.

A symphony composed in the cosmic air,
His name, a ballad beyond compare.
　With each syllable, a phoenix's flight,
James, the luminary in literature's night.
A sonnet written in the aurora's hue,
His name, an eternal rendezvous.
　So, let the quill waltz on parchment's stage,
James, the protagonist in every written page.
In the lexicon's embrace, a timeless flame,
His name, a poetry with no earthly claim.

TWENTY

JAMES, THE POET LAUREATE

In the mosaic of language, where stories intertwine,
James, a sonnet's heartbeat, a rare design.
A syllabic tapestry, intricate and bright,
His name, a celestial beacon in the poetic night.
    Beneath the canopy of metaphors, he strides,
James, the wordsmith, where eloquence abides.
A cosmic dance of consonants and vowels,
His name, a melody that gracefully howls.
    Through the chronicles of time, an epic tale,
James, the protagonist with words set sail.
A symphony of ink on the parchment's stage,
His name, an opulent verse, timeless sage.
    In the garden of expressions, a vibrant bloom,
James, the language's luminary, breaks the gloom.

A quasar of syllables, radiant and grand,
His name, a masterpiece etched in the sand.
    With each stanza, a phoenix takes flight,
James, the poet laureate, in literary light.
A constellation in the celestial dome,
His name, an anthem echoing through the poem.
    So let the metaphors waltz in rhythmic trance,
James, the storyteller, in language's expanse.
In the lexicon's embrace, an eternal flame,
His name, a symphony without a claim.

TWENTY-ONE

POETIC MASTERPIECE

In the realm of words, where narratives bloom,
James emerges, a lexicon's perfume.
A linguistic sorcerer with tales to weave,
His name, a sonnet, in the heart it cleaves.

Under the crescent moon's soft caress,
James, an enigma, in the poet's address.
A serenade sung by the midnight breeze,
His name, a stanza that gracefully frees.

Through the labyrinth of language, he strides,
James, the bard where eloquence abides.
In the cosmic dance of ink and quill,
His name, a symphony, profound and still.

In the tapestry of verses, he's the thread,
James, the balladeer where dreams are bred.
A constellation of syllables in the cosmic sea,
His name, a celestial melody.

With each stanza, a phoenix takes flight,
James, the lyricist in the poet's night.
An ode written in the ink of the stars,
His name, a universe that eternally mars.

So let the metaphors pirouette and play,
James, the artisan, in language's ballet.
In the lexicon's embrace, an eternal flame,
His name, a poetic masterpiece without a claim.

TWENTY-TWO

LOVE AND MIGHT

In realms of old and tales untold,
There lived a man with heart of gold,
James, his name, a beacon bright,
Guiding all through darkest night.
    In fields of honor, he held his ground,
A knight of virtue, true and sound,
With courage bold and spirit free,
He sailed across the endless sea.
    Through valleys deep and mountains high,
His laughter echoed to the sky,
With wisdom vast and kindness rare,
He showed the world how much to care.
    In melodies sweet, his name would ring,
A symphony of joy, a song to sing,
For James, the name that stands apart,
A masterpiece of a noble heart.

So here's to James, so pure and true,
A name that shines in every hue,
A legacy of love and might,
James, the beacon of eternal light.

TWENTY-THREE

FOREVER REIGN

In realms of dreams where shadows play,
There strides a figure, noble and fey,
James, his name, a whispered prayer,
Guardian of dreams, beyond compare.

Through mists of time and realms unseen,
He wanders where the stars convene,
With eyes that hold the secrets deep,
And promises that he will keep.

In twilight's embrace, he walks the night,
Dispelling fears with gentle might,
A champion of hope, a steadfast guide,
In James, the dreams of many reside.

His voice a melody, serene and clear,
Dispelling doubts, allaying fear,
With every step, a path he paves,
For dreamers bold and hopeful braves.

So here's to James, the dreamer's friend,
Whose name will echo without end,
In realms of fancy, and slumber's domain,
James, the guardian, shall forever reign.

TWENTY-FOUR

FOR IN JAMES

In the echoes of ages, through history's rhyme,
There strides a figure, unfathomed in time,
James, his name, a tale untold,
Voyager of time, brave and bold.
　Amidst the ruins of empires past,
He wanders where memories forever last,
With eyes that hold the wisdom's gleam,
And visions of a world unseen.
　Through ancient lands and distant shores,
He journeys on, where adventure pours,
A seeker of truth, a keeper of lore,
In James, the stories of old restore.
　His voice a whisper in the windswept air,
Carrying legends beyond compare,
With every step, a saga unfolds,
For in James, the chronicles enfold.

So here's to James, the timeless sage,
Whose name transcends every age,
In the annals of time, and history's chime,
James, the voyager, shall endure for all time.

TWENTY-FIVE

ETERNALLY BRIGHT

In the tapestry of the celestial night,
There dances a figure, adorned with starlight,
James, his name, a celestial art,
Weaving constellations with a masterful heart.

Amidst the cosmos, where galaxies twirl,
He spins the stars, a celestial swirl,
With eyes that hold the universe's gaze,
And sparks of creation in cosmic blaze.

Through nebulae and astral streams,
He paints the heavens with radiant beams,
A sculptor of worlds, a cosmic dreamer,
In James, the universe finds its gleamer.

His voice a melody, harmonizing the spheres,
Creating symphonies that transcend all fears,
With every gesture, a cosmos unfurls,
For in James, the universe whirls and swirls.

So here's to James, the celestial bard,
Whose name in the cosmos will forever guard,
In the fabric of space, and the celestial night,
James, the starlight weaver, eternally bright.

TWENTY-SIX

SANCTIFIED PLACE

In the heart of the forest, where secrets reside,
Stands a figure, steadfast with arms open wide,
James, his name, a symbol of strength,
Guardian of nature, of immeasurable length.
　Amidst the woodland's embrace, he stands tall,
A sentinel of peace, for one and for all,
With eyes that mirror the wisdom of old trees,
And roots that bind the earth as if with ease.
　Through the whispers of leaves and the rustle of boughs,
He shelters the creatures, he solemnly vows,
A protector of life, a beacon of grace,
In James, the forest finds a sacred space.
　His voice a gentle murmur in the rustling leaves,
Harmonizing with the wind that weaves,

With every breath, the forest thrives,
For in James, the woodland spirit arrives.
    So here's to James, the guardian oak,
Whose name in the forest will forever evoke,
In the heart of the woods, and the wild's embrace,
James, the guardian, a sanctified place.

TWENTY-SEVEN

DISPELS THE GLOOM

In realms of eloquence and poetic grace,
A name emerges, James, in vibrant embrace.
A symphony of syllables, a linguistic delight,
In the tapestry of language, it takes its flight.
    James, a beacon, a celestial refrain,
In the lexicon of life, it leaves its stain.
A moniker that echoes through time,
In every rhythm, in every rhyme.
    In the garden of names, a rare bloom,
James, a melody that dispels the gloom.
A constellation of letters, meticulously aligned,
In the cosmic dance, its brilliance shined.
    With echoes of valor and stories untold,
James, a legend in letters of gold.

A tapestry woven with threads so divine,
In the vast expanse of words, it does entwine.
   Celestial orbs whisper tales of the name,
James, in celestial realms, finds its fame.
A symphony of vowels and consonants so sweet,
In the poetic cosmos, it claims its seat.

TWENTY-EIGHT

BRILLIANCE ENTWINES

In the realm of nomenclature, a gem doth gleam,
James, a moniker, an ethereal dream.
A cadence of consonants, a harmonious spell,
In the mosaic of names, it rings a mellifluous bell.

James, a phoenix in the linguistic expanse,
A name that dances in the cosmic dance.
Letters intertwine, a ballet in the lexicon,
In the symphony of syllables, it plays a melodious con.

In the alchemy of language, a potion rare,
James, a sonnet woven with utmost care.
A cascade of vowels, a cascade of might,
In the labyrinth of words, it takes its flight.

A celestial echo, resonating through the ages,
James, a narrative on history's pages.

In the parchment of time, its ink does flow,
A saga of letters, an eternal glow.
   A tapestry of meaning, intricate and profound,
James, a resonance in language found.
In the eloquent parade of names, it shines,
A constellation of letters, where brilliance entwines.

TWENTY-NINE

KALEIDOSCOPE OF WORDS

In the grand tapestry of linguistic art,
A name emerges, a masterpiece, a part.
James, a symphony in syllabic grace,
An opulent melody, a linguistic embrace.
In the garden of appellations, it stands tall,
James, a sonorous echo in the naming sprawl.
A constellation of letters, a celestial rhyme,
In the poetic cosmos, it transcends time.
With consonant companions, a ballet of sound,
James, a lexiconic gem, globally renowned.
A mosaic of meaning, a linguistic spree,
In the vast expanse of words, it roams free.
Through the corridors of history, it weaves,
James, a saga of resilience it conceives.

A beacon of identity, a linguistic star,
In the boundless sky of names, it travels far.
An alphabetical dance, a linguistic ballet,
James, a lyric in the name's grand array.
A serenade of vowels and consonants aligned,
In the cosmic verse, its essence enshrined.
So, let the quill dance in its honor and glee,
James, a marvel in the linguistic sea.
In the kaleidoscope of words, a radiant flame,
A eulogy of letters, James, forever in name.

THIRTY

JAMES, WE ACCLAIM

In the lexicon's garden, a bloom unfolds,
James, a sonnet in letters, a tale retold.
A symphony of syllables, a linguistic dance,
In the poetic realm, it finds its chance.
    James, a lyrical whisper, a mellifluous tune,
In the vast repertoire of names, it's a monsoon.
Consonants and vowels waltz hand in hand,
In the linguistic ballroom, a spectacle grand.
    A cadence of meaning, profound and deep,
James, in the language's embrace, takes a leap.
A cosmic ballet of letters in motion,
In the stellar expanse, it claims its potion.
    Through time's narrative, it etches its mark,
James, a linguistic voyage, a lyrical spark.
A symposium of sounds, a celestial play,
In the anthology of names, it holds sway.

In the poetic tapestry, a vibrant thread,
James, a melody where meanings are bred.
A resonance in the linguistic choir,
In the spectrum of words, it sets a fire.
   So, let the verses sing, the quill compose,
James, a poetic sonnet that forever flows.
In the constellation of names, a shining flame,
A testament to letters, to James, we acclaim.

THIRTY-ONE

FOREVER IN NAME

In the grand symphony of language, a gem unveiled,
James, a poetic sonnet, in verses detailed.
A linguistic voyage, a kaleidoscope of sound,
In the realm of names, its glory is crowned.

James, a melody in the alphabetical dance,
A cadence of consonants, a linguistic trance.
Syllabic whispers that gracefully entwine,
In the tapestry of words, a name divine.

In the cosmic lexicon, it echoes like a hymn,
James, a celestial note in the linguistic vim.
Vowels and consonants in a harmonious blend,
In the labyrinth of language, its echoes transcend.

A narrative woven in the fabric of time,
James, a linguistic rhythm, a narrative prime.
A saga of letters, an anthem profound,
In the poetic panorama, its essence is found.

Through the corridors of history, it strides,
James, a timeless echo in linguistic tides.
A serenade of syllables, a lyrical spree,
In the expansive spectrum, it roams free.
   So, let the quill dance in honor and grace,
James, a linguistic marvel in the vast space.
In the anthology of names, a radiant flame,
A eulogy of letters, James, forever in name.

THIRTY-TWO

DANCE OF LETTERS

In the lexicon's symphony, a melody unfurls,
James, a linguistic marvel that gracefully swirls.
A ballet of syllables, a poetic trance,
In the vast domain of names, it takes a stance.

James, a sonnet written in consonants and vowels,
A tapestry of letters that eternally bow.
A linguistic echo through the corridors of time,
In the poetic landscape, it's a paradigm.

Through the alphabetic maze, it weaves its story,
James, a cadence that echoes in all its glory.
Vowels and consonants, a harmonious alliance,
In the linguistic ballet, it finds compliance.

A narrative etched in the scrolls of fate,
James, a linguistic journey that's ever ornate.
A symphonic resonance, a celestial song,
In the anthology of names, where it belongs.

In the cosmic script, a radiant script,
James, a linguistic gem, forever equipped.
A dance of letters, a lyrical flame,
In the vast expanse of words, it claims its name.
So, let the verses cascade, the quill compose,
James, a linguistic ode that forever flows.
In the constellation of names, a shining star,
A testament to letters, to James, we raise the bar.

THIRTY-THREE

RADIANT STAR

In the lexicon's ballet, a name takes flight,
James, a linguistic marvel, pure and bright.
A lyrical cascade of consonants and vowels,
In the poetic spectrum, it eternally prowls.

James, a sonnet composed in letters profound,
A symphony of syllables, a rhythmic sound.
In the grand tapestry of names, it's a refrain,
A linguistic journey, an eloquent terrain.

Through the pages of time, its tale unfolds,
James, a narrative in letters it holds.
A cadence of meaning, a celestial dance,
In the linguistic cosmos, it finds its trance.

Vowels and consonants, a harmonious blend,
James, a melody that will never end.
A cosmic resonance, a lyrical flame,
In the anthology of names, it claims its fame.

In the labyrinth of language, it marks its space,
James, a linguistic voyage, a timeless embrace.
A serenade of letters in the poetic sphere,
In the spectrum of words, it shines crystal clear.
So, let the quill dance in honor and glee,
James, a linguistic marvel in eternity.
In the constellation of names, a radiant star,
A hymn to letters, to James, we raise the bar.

THIRTY-FOUR

RARE AND FAIR

In the realm of names, a gem shines bright,
A moniker of strength and might,
James, a name with timeless grace,
In history's annals, finds its place.

From ancient lands to modern days,
James stands tall in myriad ways,
A name of kings and heroes bold,
In tales of valor, oft retold.

Like a beacon in the darkest night,
James brings hope, a guiding light,
In every heart, a flame it ignites,
A name that soars to wondrous heights.

With each syllable, a melody rings,
A symphony of noble things,
James, a name that's truly grand,
Woven into destiny's golden strand.

So let us raise our voices high,
To James, the name that paints the sky,
In every language, let it be known,
A name of power, proudly shown.

From age to age, it will endure,
A legacy strong, steadfast, and sure,
James, a name beyond compare,
A timeless emblem, rare and fair.

THIRTY-FIVE

EVERY SOUL

In the tapestry of names, one stands tall,
James, a beacon, admired by all,
A symphony of syllables, a rhythm divine,
In every echo, its brilliance will shine.

From ancient tales to modern lore,
James weaves a narrative, rich and pure,
A name of honor, a legacy grand,
In every heart, it finds its stand.

Like the oak that withstands the test of time,
James exudes strength, a truth sublime,
In the face of challenges, it stands unwavering,
A name that echoes triumph, never wavering.

From realms of art to fields of might,
James resonates with undying light,
A name that poets and bards acclaim,
In melodies of praise, it finds its fame.

So let us raise our voices in mirth,
To James, a name of immeasurable worth,
In every story, let its valor be told,
A name of eminence, timeless and bold.

In the annals of history, it etches its tale,
James, a name that will forever prevail,
In every soul, its essence embeds,
A name of reverence, as the universe spreads.

ABOUT THE AUTHOR

Walter the Educator is one of the pseudonyms for Walter Anderson. Formally educated in Chemistry, Business, and Education, he is an educator, an author, a diverse entrepreneur, and he is the son of a disabled war veteran. "Walter the Educator" shares his time between educating and creating. He holds interests and owns several creative projects that entertain, enlighten, enhance, and educate, hoping to inspire and motivate you.

Follow, find new works, and stay up to date
with Walter the Educator™
at WaltertheEducator.com

www.ingramcontent.com/pod-product-compliance
Lightning Source LLC
LaVergne TN
LVHW052000060526
838201LV00059B/3756